AF575355

THE BEGINNER'S GUIDE TO
PHYSICS
DOUGLAS HICTON
THERMODYNAMICS
LIGHTBOX
openlightbox.com

LIGHTBOX

Go to
www.openlightbox.com
and enter this book's
unique code.

ACCESS CODE

LBXS5833

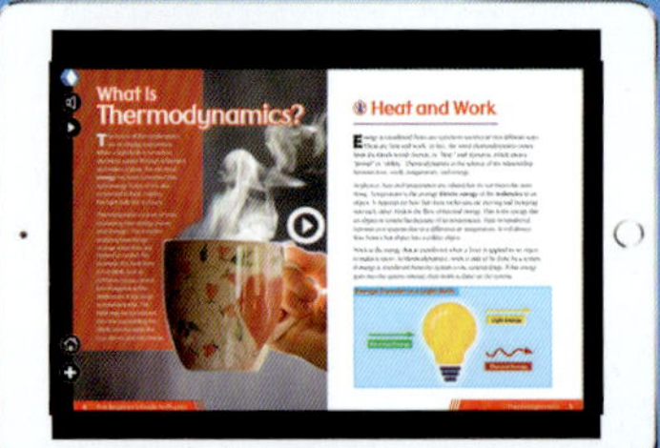

Lightbox is an all-inclusive digital solution for the teaching and learning of curriculum topics in an original, groundbreaking way. Lightbox is based on National Curriculum Standards.

LIGHTBOX SUPPLEMENTARY RESOURCES

SHARE
Share titles within your Learning Management System (LMS) or Library Circulation System

CURRICULUM
Find national and state curriculum correlations

CITATION
Create bibliographical references following APA, CMOS, and MLA styles

STANDARD FEATURES OF LIGHTBOX

AUDIO High-quality narration using text-to-speech system

ACTIVITIES Printable PDFs that can be emailed and graded

SLIDESHOWS Pictorial overviews of key concepts

VIDEOS Embedded high-definition video clips

WEBLINKS Curated links to external, child-safe resources

TRANSPARENCIES Step-by-step layering of maps, diagrams, charts, and timelines

INTERACTIVE MAPS Interactive maps and aerial satellite imagery

QUIZZES Ten multiple-choice questions that are automatically graded and emailed for teacher assessment

KEY WORDS Matching key concepts to their definitions

This title is part of our Lightbox digital subscription

Lightbox Grades 6–8 Subscription
ISBN 978-1-5105-6068-0

Access hundreds of Lightbox titles with our digital subscription. Sign up for a **FREE** subscription trial at **www.openlightbox.com/trial**

The digital components of this book are guaranteed to stay active for at least five years from the date of publication.

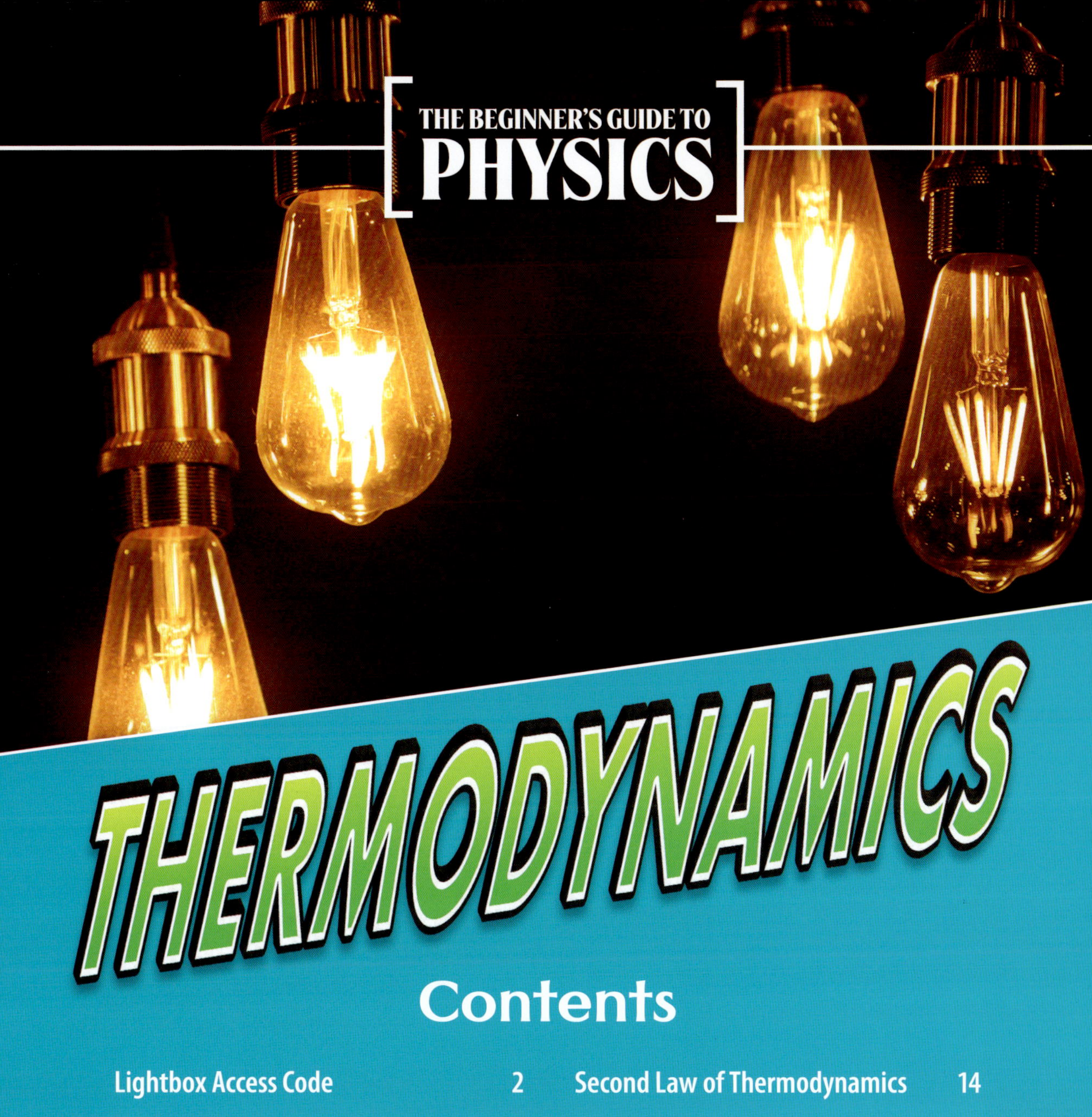

THERMODYNAMICS

Contents

Lightbox Access Code	2
What Is Thermodynamics?	4
Heat and Work	5
Thermodynamic Systems	6
Entropy	8
Temperature	9
Thermodynamics around the World	10
Zeroth Law of Thermodynamics	12
First Law of Thermodynamics	13
Second Law of Thermodynamics	14
Third Law of Thermodynamics	15
Thermodynamics through the Ages	16
Pioneers of Thermodynamics	18
What Is an HVAC Technician?	20
Science in Action	21
Quiz	22
Key Words/Index	23
Log on to www.openlightbox.com	24

What Is Thermodynamics?

The forces of thermodynamics are on display everywhere. When a light bulb is turned on, electricity travels into it and makes it glow. The electrical **energy** has been converted into light energy. Some of it is also converted to heat, making the light bulb hot to touch.

Thermodynamics explains how energy moves and transforms. This includes how things change when they are heated or cooled. For example, the heat from a hot drink, such as coffee or cocoa, cannot just disappear as the drink cools. It has to go somewhere else. The heat is transferred into the cup holding the drink, into the table the cup sits on, and into the air.

Heat and Work

In thermodynamics, a system refers to a specific object or group of objects being studied. Energy is transferred from one system to another in two different ways. These are heat and work. In fact, the word *thermodynamics* comes from the Greek words *therme*, or "heat," and *dynamis*, which means "power" or "ability." Thermodynamics is the science of the relationship between heat, work, temperature, and energy.

Heat and temperature are related concepts in physics, but do not mean the same thing. Temperature is the average **kinetic energy** of the **molecules** in an object. It depends on how fast these molecules are moving and bumping into each other. Heat is the flow of thermal energy. This is the energy that a system has because of its temperature. Heat is transferred between two systems due to a difference in temperature. It will always flow from a hot system into a colder system.

Work is the energy that is transferred when a force is applied to a system to make it move. In thermodynamics, work is said to be done by a system if energy is transferred from the system to its surroundings. If the energy goes into the system instead, then work is done on the system.

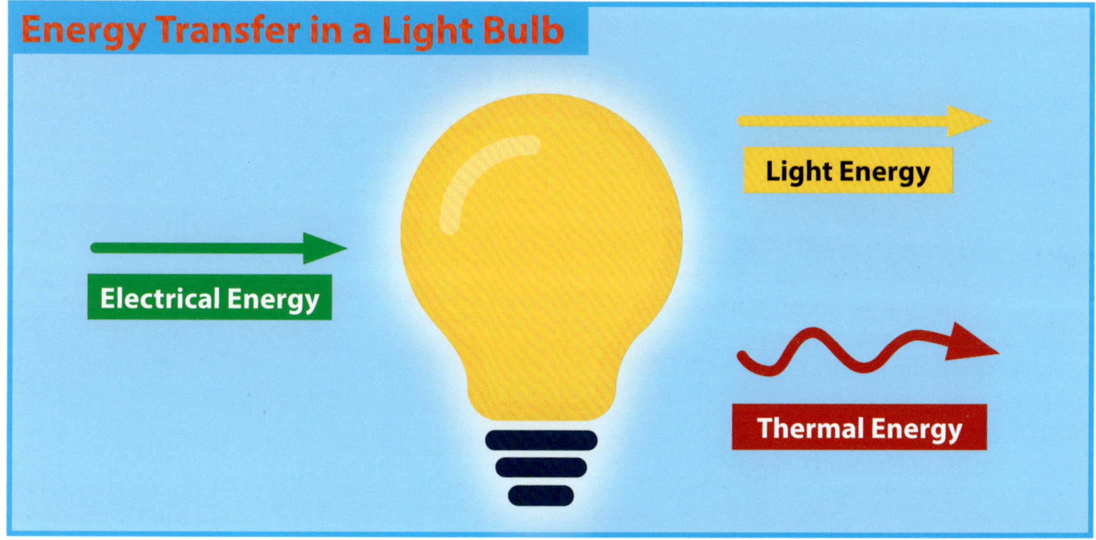

Thermodynamic Systems

A thermodynamic system is separated from its surroundings by a boundary. The three types of thermodynamic systems are open, closed, and isolated. They differ in how **matter** and energy are exchanged between the system and its surroundings.

Open System

Both energy and matter can flow in and out of an open system. An uncovered pot of boiling water on a stove is an example of an open system. Heat is transferred from the stove to the pot, causing the water to boil and **evaporate** into water vapor. The water vapor escapes from the system into the surrounding air.

Plants and animals are also open systems. They consume chemical energy in the form of food. Then, they release waste products and heat.

Heat from a stove enters a pot of water through a method of heat transfer called conduction.

Over time, the water in a hot-water bottle becomes colder. This is because it is transferring its heat into its surroundings.

Closed System

A closed system can only exchange energy with its surroundings. Matter cannot enter or leave. A sealed hot-water bottle is a type of closed system. It can transfer heat, but no air or water can move in or out.

Earth can also be considered a closed system. Its atmosphere keeps out matter but lets energy from the Sun enter and warm the planet. The atmosphere also allows some energy to escape back into space so that the planet does not overheat.

Knowing the difference between these systems allows scientists to predict how a system will behave and how much energy it will absorb or produce. Understanding heat transfer in an open system helps engineers build engines that waste less energy. Studying energy transfer in a closed system lets scientists design better **insulating** materials.

Isolated System

An isolated system exchanges neither energy nor matter with its surroundings. It is completely **self-contained** and does not interact with anything outside of itself. In the real world, it is difficult to create a truly isolated system.

A thermos is often used as an example of an isolated system. It is designed to keep things hot or cold without letting heat escape. Any liquid inside a thermos will remain hot for a long time because it is not exchanging heat with the environment outside.

The universe as a whole can be thought of as an isolated system, too. It contains all the matter and energy that exists. This means that there is nothing to enter or leave it.

Bomb calorimeters are isolated systems found in some science laboratories. Scientists use them to measure the heat released when a substance is burned.

Entropy

Entropy (S) measures the disorder or **randomness** in a system. This is the amount of energy that is not available to do work. A highly ordered system has low entropy, while a very disordered system has high entropy. Gases have much higher entropy than solids and liquids. The molecules in gases are very far apart, which means they have the freedom to move around and arrange themselves in random ways.

When energy is transformed, entropy also changes. In some reactions, the entropy of a system increases. Energy spreads out in all directions and become less usable. For example, solid firewood has highly usable energy. Once it is burned in a campfire, the wood is transformed into smoke, ash, and gases, such as carbon dioxide. These spread energy outward, where it is no longer usable.

The entropy of open and closed systems can also decrease or increase as they interact with their surroundings. However, the entropy of an isolated system either increases or stays the same over time (t). It can never decrease. This is because entropy naturally increases over time, while an input of energy is needed to decrease the disorder in a system.

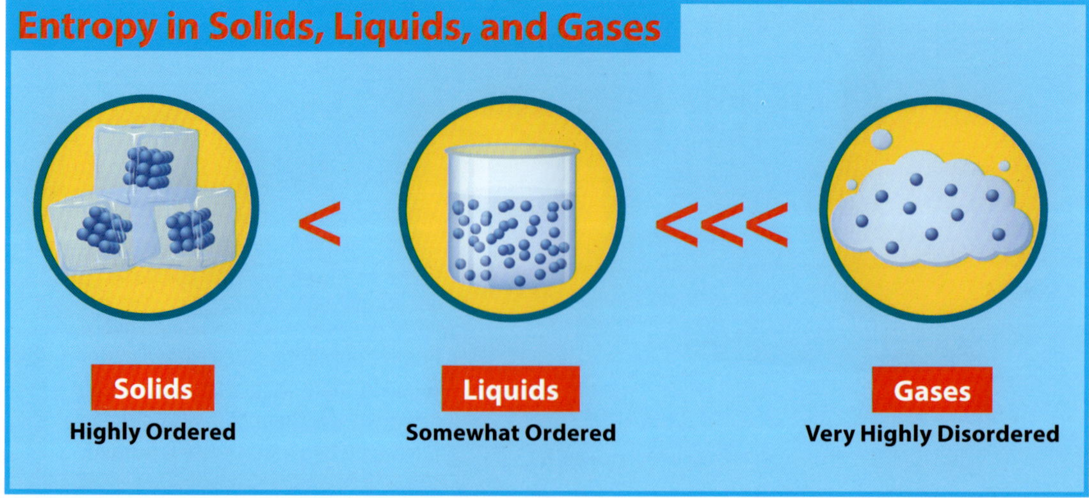

Temperature

Entropy is influenced by temperature. The lower the temperature of a system, the lower its entropy. Objects at a low temperature have low kinetic energy, which means their molecules move slowly. This reduces the disorder in a given object or group of objects.

There are different scales used to measure temperature. The most common are the Fahrenheit, Celsius, and Kelvin scales. The Fahrenheit temperature scale is mainly used in the United States, while most other countries use Celsius. Scientists often use the Kelvin scale.

One reason why scientists use the Kelvin scale is that it begins at 0 kelvin. Also called absolute zero, this is the lowest possible temperature in the universe. Starting from 0 kelvin makes measurements easier, since there is no need to use negative temperatures. Absolute zero is equal to -273.15° Celsius, or -459.67° Fahrenheit. Nothing that people have observed has ever reached absolute zero, but scientists have achieved temperatures that are very close.

Comparing Temperature Scales

A kelvin (K) and a degree Celsius (°C) are the same size. They are both 1.8 times larger than a degree Fahrenheit (°F).

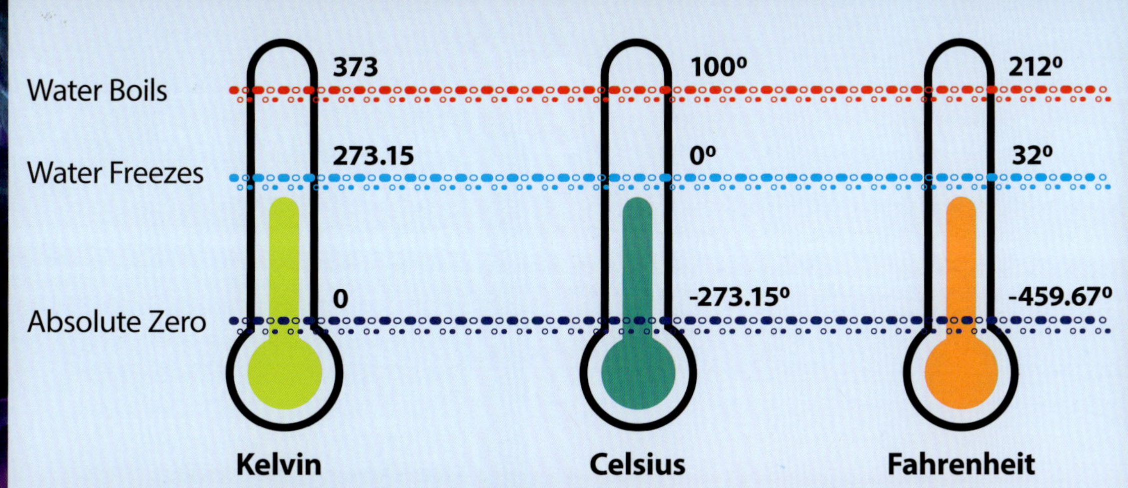

Thermodynamics around the World

Almost all of Earth's energy comes from the Sun. Like other stars, the Sun is powered by nuclear **fusion**, which generates a tremendous amount of energy. Scientists are working to learn more about nuclear fusion. In the future, it could be used as a source of clean, renewable energy.

Solar panels are one way to harness the Sun's energy. This energy can then be transformed into electricity. Electricity provides people around the world with light and power. It is also used in heating and cooling systems. Electricity can even be used to create very powerful magnets called electromagnets.

Scientists are always looking for ways to make energy conversion more efficient. For example, electricity is conducted more easily by cold metals than hot metals. The field of cryogenics studies how systems behave at extremely low temperatures.

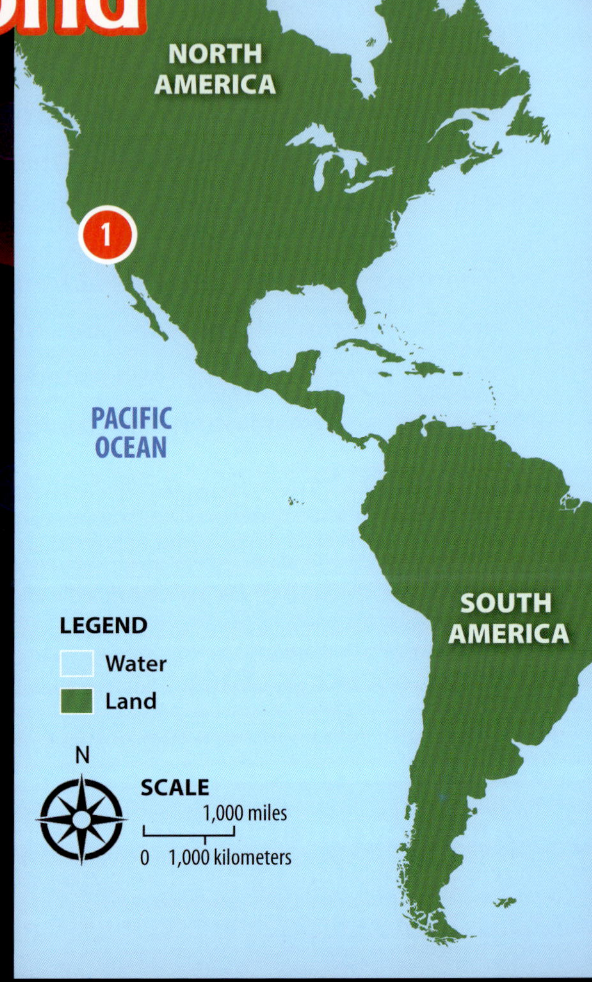

1 First Successful Fusion Ignition

Livermore, California, United States

In December 2022, scientists at the Lawrence Livermore National Laboratory used lasers to join, or fuse, hydrogen atoms together. It was the first time a fusion reaction done by people released more energy than the experiment consumed, making fusion a possible clean energy source for the future.

2 Concentrated Solar Power Plant

Ouarzazate, Morocco

Concentrated solar power systems use mirrors and lenses to help harness the Sun's energy. The Ouarzazate Solar Power Station has thousands of mirrors. It provides electricity to more than 1 million people.

3 Largest Cryogenic System

Geneva, Switzerland

The Large Hadron Collider, a particle collider at the CERN laboratory, uses extremely cold electromagnets to conduct large electrical currents. The magnets are cooled by liquid helium to -456°F (-271°C). This temperature is so cold that they do not generate heat or lose energy.

4 District Cooling Technology at Work

Singapore

Singapore's Marina Bay district is cooled through a modern energy-saving technique called district cooling. Central cooling plants send chilled water to multiple buildings. When the water heats up, it is sent back to the cooling plant, chilled again, and recirculated.

Zeroth Law of Thermodynamics

The zeroth law of thermodynamics states that if two objects are in thermal equilibrium with a third object, they must also be in thermal equilibrium with each other. Thermal equilibrium means that two objects or systems have the same temperature.

In mathematics, if A = B and B = C, then A = C. The same applies in thermodynamics. If A is the same temperature as B, and B is the same temperature as C, then logically A will be the same temperature as C. All these systems are in thermal equilibrium.

Thermometers

Thermometers are tools that measure temperature. The fluid inside a liquid thermometer expands when heated and contracts when cooled. A thermometer is an example of a closed system. The fluid inside the instrument does not leave, but it is still affected by the energy that acts on it. If a thermometer measures the same temperature in two other systems, then all three systems are in thermal equilibrium.

Why "Zeroth"?

The zeroth law of thermodynamics was discovered years after the other three laws had already been established. It was named the zeroth law instead of the fourth law because it is considered an even more basic principle than the others. It needs to be understood before the other laws can be properly applied.

First Law of Thermodynamics

The first law of thermodynamics explains the **conservation** of energy. It states that energy can never be created or destroyed, only changed from one form to another. The total amount of energy in the universe always stays the same.

For example, a ball held at the top of a steep hill has a large amount of potential, or stored, energy. Once the ball is dropped and starts rolling down the hill, the potential energy changes to kinetic energy, or the energy of motion. Energy is being transformed, not lost or gained. As the ball rolls down, its potential energy decreases while its kinetic energy increases.

Energy is conserved in all processes, whether they are natural, such as the water cycle, or artificial, such as car engines. The principles behind the first law of thermodynamics allow scientists to understand how energy is transferred and transformed in different systems. It also helps them to design processes that use less energy.

$\Delta U = Q - W$

The first law of thermodynamics can also be written in an equation form. In mathematics and physics, the Δ symbol means "change."

The equation is $\Delta U = Q - W$, where:

- ΔU = change in internal energy of a system
- Q = heat added to the system
- W = work done by the system

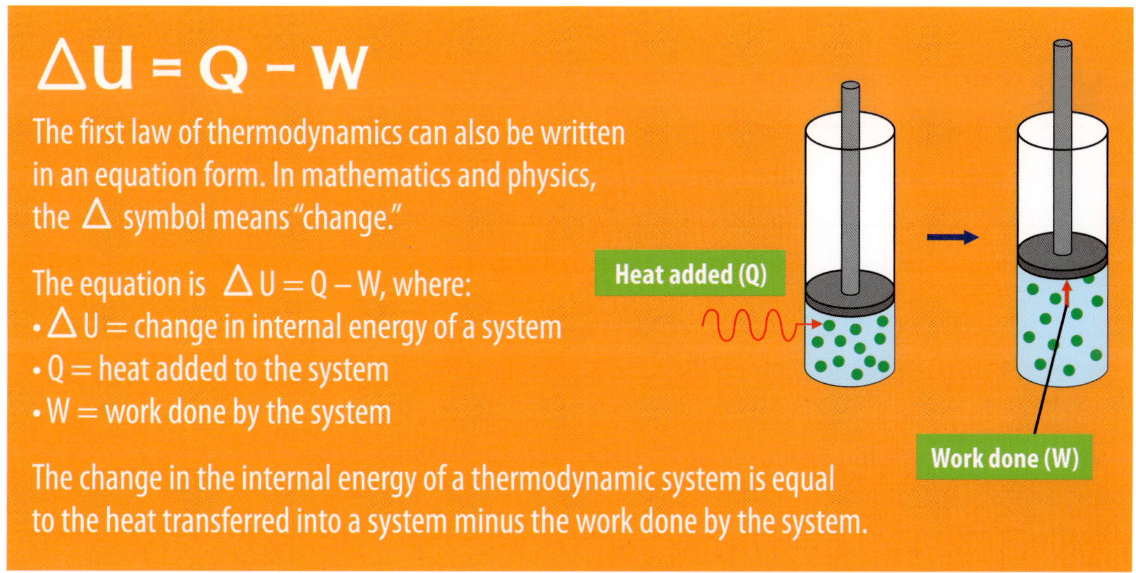

The change in the internal energy of a thermodynamic system is equal to the heat transferred into a system minus the work done by the system.

Second Law of Thermodynamics

The second law of thermodynamics states that the entropy of the universe is always increasing. When energy is transformed, some of it becomes unavailable to do work. Every energy transformation is **inefficient**. This means that some energy is always lost in an unusable form, such as heat.

One example of the second law of thermodynamics in action is a basketball that is dropped from a height. When it hits the ground, it bounces back up. With each bounce, however, the ball loses some energy due to **friction** and **air resistance**. Each bounce is smaller than the previous one. Eventually, the ball loses all its energy and comes to a complete stop.

Entropy increases over time, while usable energy decreases. It becomes more difficult to use that energy again. Because some energy is always lost as heat, it is impossible to create a machine that is 100 percent efficient at converting energy into work.

Perpetual Motion, an Impossible Dream

A perpetual motion machine is an appealing idea. It promises an endless supply of energy with no need to refuel. Some of the best-known attempts to build perpetual motion machines were by Robert Boyle in the 1600s and Johann Bessler in the 1700s.

However, none of these machines worked. Perpetual motion machines violate the first and second laws of thermodynamics. They require the machines to create more energy than they use, which is not possible, since energy cannot be created or destroyed. Factors such as friction and air resistance cause energy to be lost from a system over time, making it impossible for a machine to operate forever.

Third Law of Thermodynamics

As the temperature of a system approaches absolute zero, the entropy of the system also approaches zero. At absolute zero, there is absolutely no energy, molecular motion, or entropy. Since there is no thermal energy, there is nothing to cause any movement or disorder. According to the third law of thermodynamics, the entropy of a pure, **crystalline** substance is equal to zero at absolute zero.

At very low temperatures, the atoms that make up matter begin to line up in a very specific way. At absolute zero, they would be perfectly lined up and would not move at all. This is called the "ground state" of the system.

The third law of thermodynamics is often used to explain why certain materials behave the way they do at extremely low temperatures. It has important applications in science and technology, including in fields such as cryogenics. Superconductors, for instance, are materials that can conduct electricity extremely well when cooled to very low temperatures.

Overview of the Laws of Thermodynamics

Together, the laws of thermodynamics explain the changes in energy.

0	Zeroth Law	If **A=B** and **B=C**, then **A=C**	Two systems in thermal equilibrium with a third system are also in thermal equilibrium with each other.
1	First Law	$\Delta U = Q - W$	Energy cannot be created or destroyed, only changed from one form to another.
2	Second Law	$\Delta S / \Delta t \geq 0$	The entropy of the universe is always increasing with time.
3	Third Law	**S = 0** at **0 Kelvin**	The entropy of a pure substance is zero at absolute zero.

Thermodynamics through the Ages

Thermodynamics as a scientific field of study only goes back about 200 years. However, the principles behind thermodynamic processes have been used by people for thousands of years. From sailboats to steam engines to superconductors, the transfer of energy between different forms has powered many technologies.

62 AD

Heron of Alexandria, a Greek scientist, invents the aeolipile. This is a steam-powered device with a spinning sphere. Steam enters the aeolipile and rushes out through two bent tubes, making it rotate. It is used to show people how heat can be turned into motion.

1769

The steam engine is improved by James Watt, a Scottish inventor. His work plays an important role in helping scientists understand how energy can be transformed and transferred.

1824

French engineer and physicist Nicolas Léonard Sadi Carnot publishes *Reflections on the* ***Motive*** *Power of Fire*. This paper lays the foundation for the first and second laws of thermodynamics.

1845

James Prescott Joule, a physicist from England, publishes a paper exploring the relationship between heat and mechanical work.

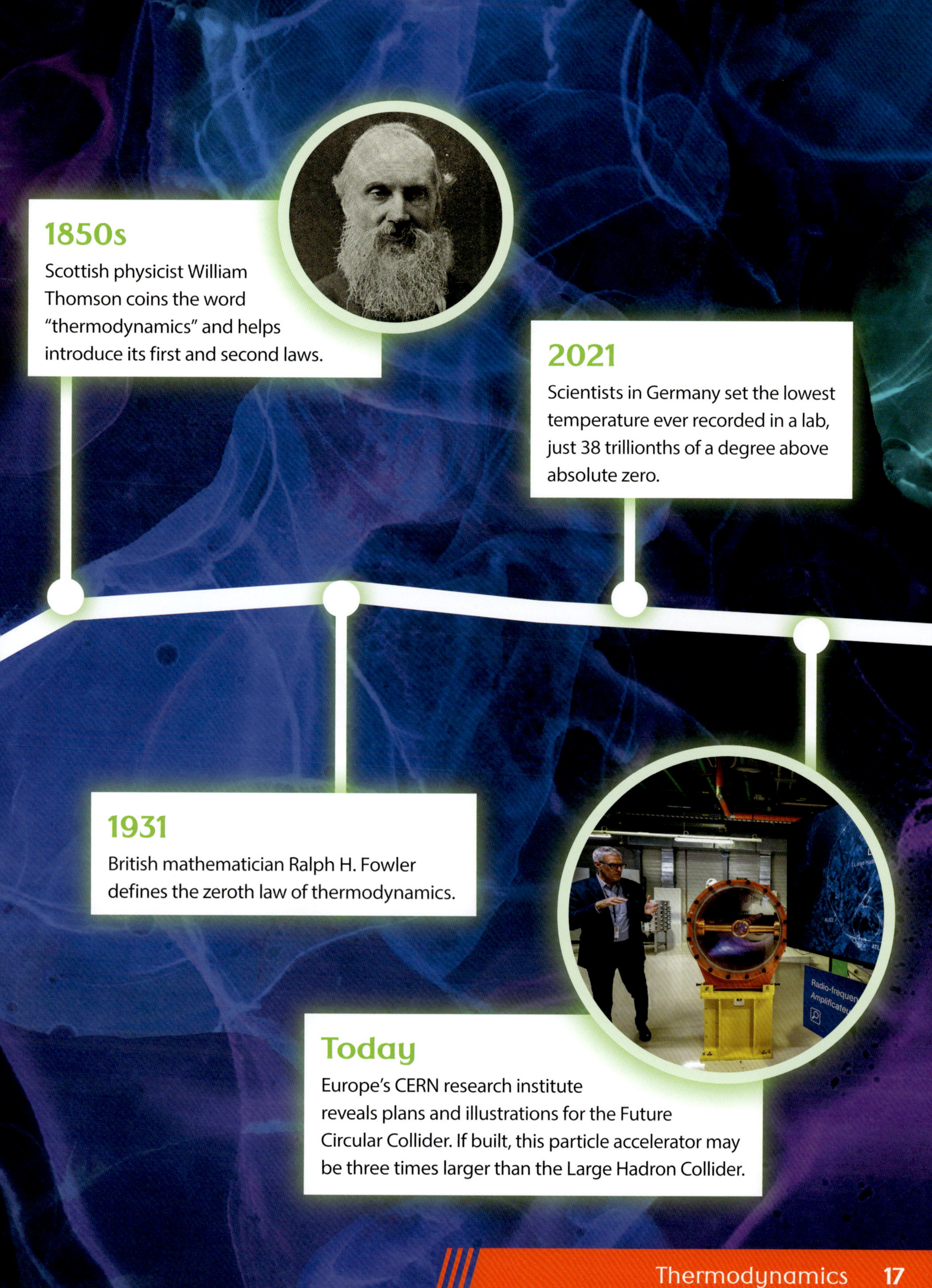

1850s

Scottish physicist William Thomson coins the word "thermodynamics" and helps introduce its first and second laws.

2021

Scientists in Germany set the lowest temperature ever recorded in a lab, just 38 trillionths of a degree above absolute zero.

1931

British mathematician Ralph H. Fowler defines the zeroth law of thermodynamics.

Today

Europe's CERN research institute reveals plans and illustrations for the Future Circular Collider. If built, this particle accelerator may be three times larger than the Large Hadron Collider.

Pioneers of Thermodynamics

Nicolas Léonard Sadi Carnot

(1796–1832)

Nicolas Léonard Sadi Carnot is known as the "Father of Thermodynamics." Interested from a young age in industrial engineering, he served in the French Army as a military engineer until 1814. In the 1820s, Carnot focused on the steam engine. He soon identified some of its limitations. His 1824 *Reflections on the Motive Power of Fire* publication was considered the founding work of thermodynamics. "Motive power" was Carnot's term for work, and "fire" was used for heat. Carnot also developed the concept of the Carnot cycle, a **theoretical** cycle that describes how heat engines work.

James Prescott Joule

(1818–1889)

James Prescott Joule's "On the Mechanical Equivalent of Heat" paper laid the foundation for the theory of conservation of energy. Joule conducted experiments to determine the mechanical equivalent of heat. They showed that heat and work are both forms of energy. His work with Lord Kelvin on the absolute scale of temperature and the Joule-Thomson effect contributed to the development of refrigeration. The most commonly used unit of energy, the Joule, is named after him. Joule was elected to the Royal Society of London and received the prestigious Royal Medal award for his work.

William Thomson

(1824–1907)

William Thomson made significant contributions to the study of both thermodynamics and electricity. He was knighted and became known as Lord Kelvin. Thomson began studying at the University of Glasgow at the age of 10, and eventually went on to become a professor there. He proposed the absolute temperature scale that was later named the Kelvin scale. His essay, "On the Dynamical Theory of Heat," contained his version of the second law of thermodynamics.

Carnot Cycle

Engines in cars, turbines, and other machines always lose some energy to heat. In real life, no engine can be 100 percent efficient. The Carnot cycle is an **idealized** version of an engine. It describes the most efficient way to turn heat into work. The four steps of the Carnot cycle happen in a loop.

Step 1

A gas is heated at a constant temperature while it expands. **Isothermal** expansion allows the gas to do work on its surroundings.

Step 2

The gas expands further without exchanging any heat with its surroundings. **Adiabatic** expansion leads to the gas cooling down.

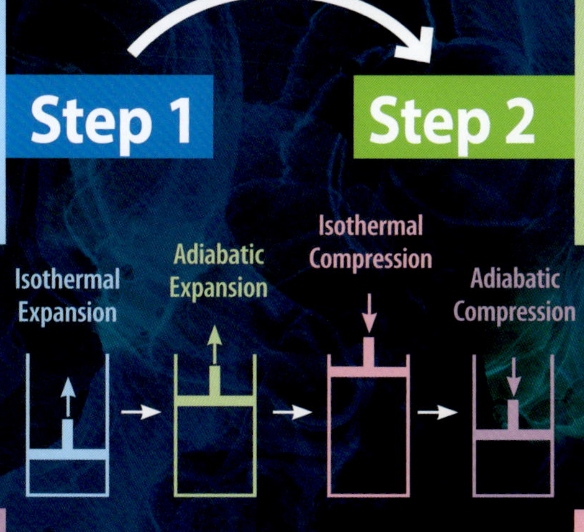

Step 3

The gas is cooled at a constant temperature while it is compressed. It releases energy into its surroundings as a result of isothermal compression.

Step 4

The gas is compressed further without exchanging any heat with its surroundings. Adiabatic compression causes the gas to heat up.

What Is an HVAC Technician?

Heating, ventilation, and air conditioning (HVAC) technicians work with heating and cooling systems. They install, maintain, and repair heaters, air conditioners, and more. HVAC technicians must have a good understanding of the four main types of heating and air circulation systems. These are split, hybrid, duct-free, and packaged HVAC systems.

Inspecting HVAC systems and fixing problems with them is a large part of the job. HVAC technicians need to be able to interpret blueprints and technical manuals. Since they often deal with clients face-to-face, they should also be good at customer service. Some jobs only take a few hours, while others last days.

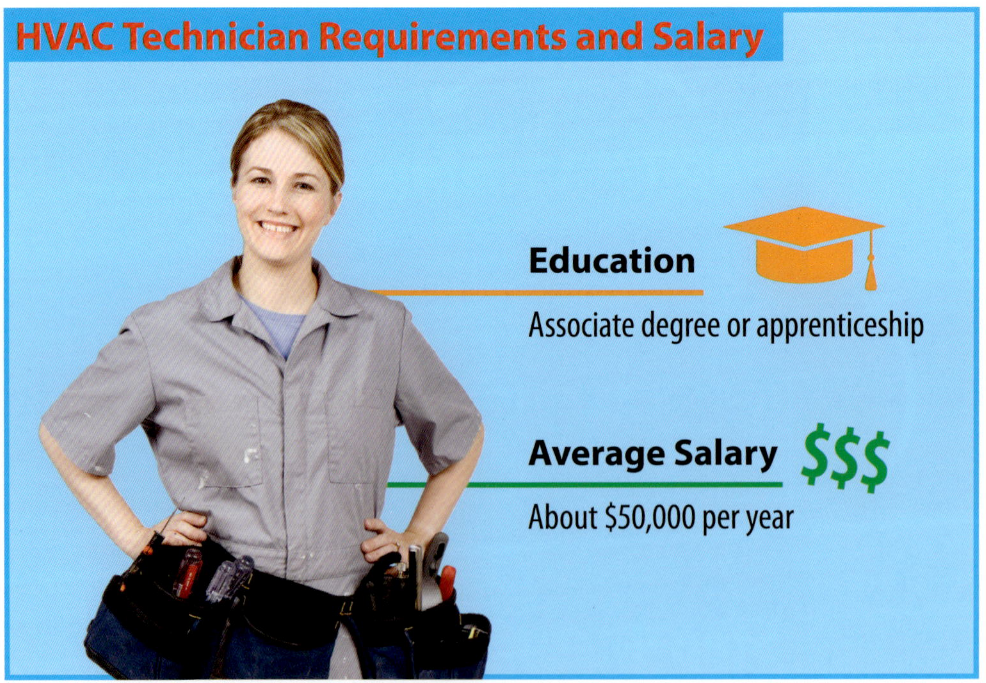

Science in Action

Inflating a Balloon

Materials

- one balloon
- one empty plastic bottle
- white vinegar
- baking soda
- measuring cup or spoons

Directions

1. Pour about ½ cup (120 milliliters) of vinegar into the plastic bottle. Pour ¼ cup tablespoons (60 ml) of baking soda into the balloon.

2. Carefully stretch the opening of the balloon over the bottle's neck. It should be sealed well so that no air can enter in or out. Be careful not to let any baking soda fall into the bottle yet.

3. Lift the balloon and allow the baking soda to pour into the bottle. It will mix with the vinegar.

4. Observe as the reaction occurs and the balloon inflates.

WHY DOES THIS HAPPEN?

Both the vinegar and the baking soda have chemical potential energy. As the two substances mix, a chemical reaction produces carbon dioxide gas. The gas rises and inflates the balloon.

This experiment demonstrates the first law of thermodynamics, which focuses on energy conservation. The chemical potential energy is transformed into kinetic energy. The movement and resulting expansion of the gas molecules causes the balloon to inflate.

1. Where does the name *thermodynamics* come from?
2. Where is the Large Hadron Collider located?
3. Which law of thermodynamics was the last to be discovered?
4. What are the three types of systems in thermodynamics?
5. What temperature is absolute zero in the Kelvin, Fahrenheit, and Celsius scales?
6. Which law states that energy cannot be created or destroyed?
7. Who is referred to as the "Father of Thermodynamics"?
8. What is disorder or randomness in a system called?
9. Which scientist coined the word "thermodynamics"?
10. What does the second law of thermodynamics state?

ANSWERS

1. From the Greek words *therme*, or "heat," and *dynamis*, which means "power" or "ability" 2. Geneva, Switzerland 3. The zeroth law 4. Open, closed, and isolated systems 5. 0 K, -459.67°F, and -273.15°C 6. The first law of thermodynamics 7. Nicolas Léonard Sadi Carnot 8. Entropy 9. William Thomson (Lord Kelvin) 10. The entropy of the universe is always increasing

Key Words

adiabatic: when heat does not enter or leave a system

air resistance: the force that air exerts against a moving object, slowing it down

conservation: when the energy in a closed system remains constant

crystalline: a tightly packed and highly ordered solid

energy: the ability to do work

evaporate: change from a liquid to a gas

friction: the force that slows down one solid object moving over another

fusion: a nuclear reaction that releases energy by joining the nuclei of two atoms

idealized: seen as perfect or better than is possible in reality

inefficient: not achieving the maximum possible productivity

insulating: able to reduce the amount of energy entering or leaving a system

isothermal: happening at a temperature that does not change

kinetic energy: the energy that a moving object has because of its motion

matter: anything that has mass and takes up space, such as solids, liquids, and gases

molecules: groups of atoms bonded together that make up the smallest unit of matter

motive: causing something to move

randomness: unpredictability and lack of a pattern

self-contained: independent, complete, and not influenced by anything else

theoretical: existing only as an idea and not in reality

Index

absolute zero 9, 15, 17, 22

Carnot, Nicolas Léonard Sadi 16, 18, 22
closed system 6, 7, 8, 12, 22

entropy 8, 9, 14, 15, 22

first law of thermodynamics 13, 14, 15, 16, 17, 21, 22

isolated system 6, 7, 8, 22

Joule, James Prescott 16, 18

open system 6, 7, 8, 22

perpetual motion 14

second law of thermodynamics 14, 15, 16, 17, 19, 22

thermal equilibrium 12, 15
third law of thermodynamics 15
Thomson, William (Lord Kelvin) 17, 19, 22

zeroth law of thermodynamics 12, 15, 17, 22

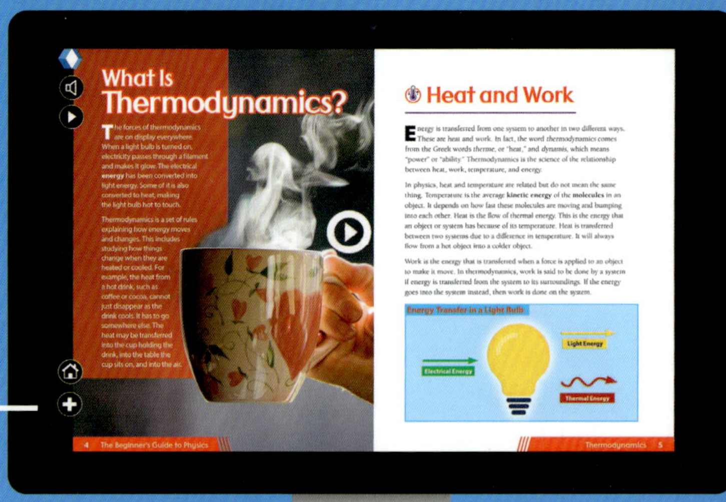

SUPPLEMENTARY RESOURCES

Click on the plus icon found in the bottom left corner of each spread to open additional teacher resources.

- Download and print the book's quizzes and activities
- Access curriculum correlations
- Explore additional web applications that enhance the Lightbox experience

LIGHTBOX DIGITAL TITLES
Packed full of integrated media

VIDEOS

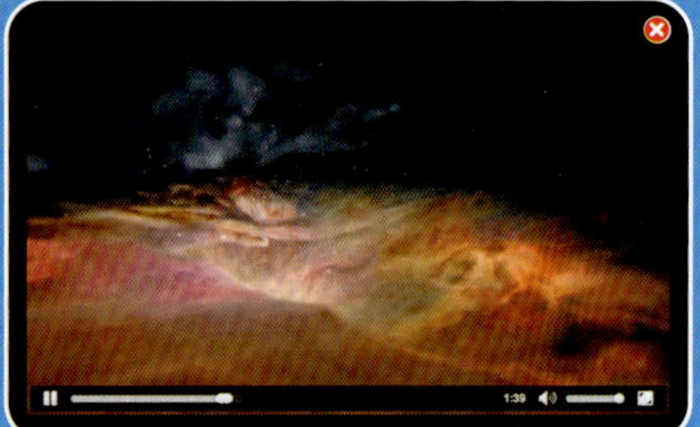

INTERACTIVE MAPS

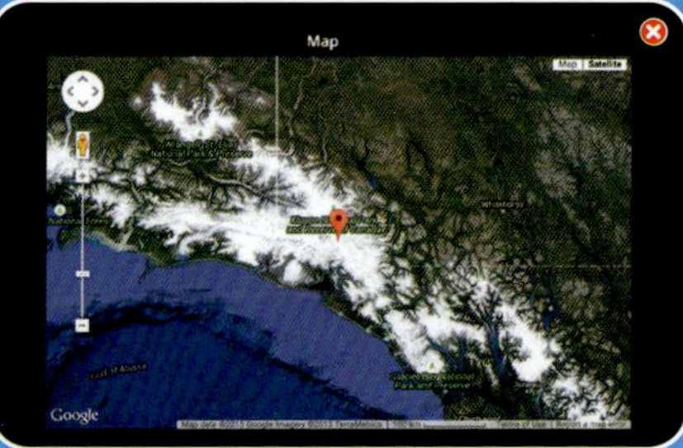

WEBLINKS

SLIDESHOWS

QUIZZES

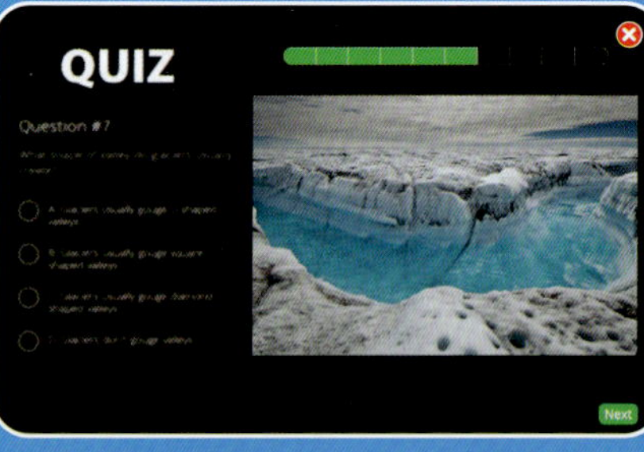

OPTIMIZED FOR
- ✓ TABLETS
- ✓ SMART BOARDS
- ✓ COMPUTERS
- ✓ AND MUCH MORE!

Published by Lightbox Learning Inc.
276 5th Avenue, Suite 704 #917
New York, NY 10001
Website: www.openlightbox.com

Copyright ©2025 Lightbox Learning Inc.
All rights reserved. No part of this publication may be reproduced, stored in a retrieval system, or transmitted in any form or by any means, electronic, mechanical, photocopying, recording, or otherwise, without the prior written permission of the publisher.

Library of Congress Control Number: 2024936221

ISBN 978-1-5105-6710-8 (hardcover)
ISBN 978-1-5105-6711-5 (multi-user static eBook)
ISBN 978-1-5105-8088-6 (multi-user interactive eBook)

Printed in Guangzhou, China
1 2 3 4 5 6 7 8 9 0 28 27 26 25 24

062024
111023

Project Coordinator Priyanka Das
Designer Mandy Christiansen

Photo Credits
Every reasonable effort has been made to trace ownership and to obtain permission to reprint copyright material. The publisher would be pleased to have any errors or omissions brought to its attention so that they may be corrected in subsequent printings.

The publisher acknowledges Getty Images and Shutterstock as its primary image suppliers for this title.